The Life and
JESUS CHRIST

# Following
# Jesus

NAVPRESS
BRINGING TRUTH TO LIFE
NavPress Publishing Group
P.O. Box 35001, Colorado Springs, Colorado 80935

The Navigators is an international Christian organization. Our mission is to reach, disciple, and equip people to know Christ and to make Him known through successive generations. We envision multitudes of diverse people in the United States and every other nation who have a passionate love for Christ, live a lifestyle of sharing Christ's love, and multiply spiritual laborers among those without Christ.

NavPress is the publishing ministry of The Navigators. NavPress publications help believers learn biblical truth and apply what they learn to their lives and ministries. Our mission is to stimulate spiritual formation among our readers.

Map: GeoSystems Global Corporation

This series was produced for NavPress with the assistance of The Livingstone Corporation. James C. Galvin, Valerie Weidemann, and Daryl J. Lucas, project editors.

Unless otherwise identified, all Scripture quotations in this publication are taken from the *HOLY BIBLE: NEW INTERNATIONAL VERSION* ® (NIV®). Copyright © 1973, 1978, 1984 by International Bible Society. Used by permission of Zondervan Publishing House.

Printed in the United States of America

2 3 4 5 6 7 8 9 10 11 12 13 14 15 /05 04 03 02 01 00 99 98

---

FOR A FREE CATALOG OF
NAVPRESS BOOKS & BIBLE STUDIES,
CALL 1-800-366-7788 (USA)
or 1-416-499-4615 (CANADA)

# CONTENTS

Study guides in the
LIFE AND MINISTRY OF JESUS CHRIST series:

*The Beginning*
*Challenging Tradition*
*The Messiah*
*Following Jesus*
*Answering the Call*
*Final Teachings*
*The Cross and Resurrection*

# INTRODUCTION

If you want to learn more about Jesus Christ and become more like Him, then THE LIFE AND MINISTRY OF JESUS CHRIST series is for you and your small group. This seven-book Bible study spans all four Gospels, covers the entire life of Christ in chronological order, and emphasizes personal application of biblical truth. By using an inductive study format, THE LIFE AND MINISTRY OF JESUS CHRIST helps you investigate for yourself what Jesus did and what He taught.

Each guide has five lessons and may be studied in five sessions, or in as many as ten to twelve sessions if your group prefers a slower pace. For best results, each group member should study the passages listed and write out the answers to the questions—including the application questions in the side columns. Then, as you meet with your Bible study group or class you can discuss what you have observed and applied. Use the side columns to write out any additional insights or applications that emerge from the discussion. The emphasis on application helps to maintain a balance between factual knowledge and character development. The more time and prayer you invest in the study, the more you will gain from it.

In each section of a given lesson, one biblical passage will be the main focus of study. That passage is printed out for you. Additional passages may also be listed. Read them as you have time.

A separate leader's resource guide is available for THE LIFE AND MINISTRY OF JESUS CHRIST series that provides additional background for each lesson and optional discussion questions for the group.

The Scripture passages were arranged based on the order presented by A. T. Robertson in *A Harmony of the Gospels* (Harper & Brothers, 1950). A harmony is a sequencing of the four Gospel accounts of the life of Jesus in parallel form to facilitate a study of His life and ministry. You can find the harmony used in this study in the "Harmony of the Life and Ministry of Jesus Christ" in the back of each study guide.

A harmony shows the events in the life of Christ in chronological order. Some events, such as the feeding of the five thousand, are recorded in all four gospels; others, such as Jesus' interview with Nicodemus in the Gospel of John, appear in only one. Mark's Gospel is the most chronological; Matthew's follows themes more closely than chronology.

Without careful study and the aid of a harmony, the Gospels may appear to contain chronological discrepancies. The order of the material in each Gospel differs because Jesus taught the same truths, told the same parables, and performed similar miracles many times in His three-and-a-half year ministry. So Matthew recorded the contents of the Sermon on the Mount in one large section toward the beginning of Jesus' ministry (Matthew 5–7), while Luke wrote down similar teachings of Jesus throughout His ministry (Luke 6:17-49, 11:1-13, 13:22-30). Undoubtedly Jesus pronounced judgment on those who opposed and harassed Him a number of times, so Matthew tells of an incident in Galilee toward the middle of His ministry (Matthew 12:22-45) while Luke records another such confrontation, this time in Judea, later in His ministry (Luke 11:14-36). These are not contradictions but records of similar events.

This Bible study resulted from the diligent work of many men and women around the world. A team of Navigator staff realized the need for this study and began putting it together. Others field tested the material and made refinements. Still others read it and offered valuable advice. Then skilled editors shaped the study to its final form.

To all who have prayed and labored diligently, a hearty word of thanks. It is, in every sense, the result of a team effort, coached and coordinated by the Holy Spirit. As the Author of the Word of God, as Teacher and Interpreter of the Word to believers, and as the Divine Distributor of His gifts to them, the Holy Spirit has in a unique way directed the production of this study. His desire for its effectiveness must stem from His special ministry of revealing and glorifying Jesus Christ in our lives. To this purpose the study is dedicated.

*"I have much more to say to you, more than you can now bear. But when he, the Spirit of truth, comes, he will guide you into all truth. He will not speak on his own; he will speak only what he hears, and he will tell you what is yet to come. He will bring glory to me by taking from what is mine and making it known to you. All that belongs to the Father is mine. That is why I said the Spirit will take from what is mine and make it known to you." (John 16:12-15)*

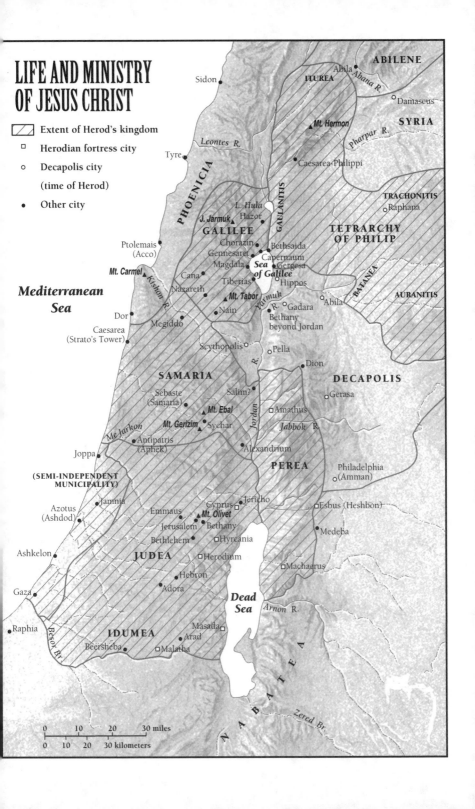

# LIFE AND MINISTRY OF JESUS CHRIST

- ▨ Extent of Herod's kingdom
- ⬛ Herodian fortress city
- ○ Decapolis city
  (time of Herod)
- ● Other city

**Mediterranean Sea**

ABILENE

Abila
ITUREA      Abana R.
Sidon

○ Damascus

SYRIA

▲ Mt. Hermon

Pharpar R.

Leontes R.

Tyre

Caesarea-Philippi

PHOENICIA

GAULANITIS

TRACHONITIS
○ Raphana

L. Hula
Hazor
J. Jarmuk

GALILEE

TETRARCHY
OF PHILIP

Chorazin
Ptolemais      Gennesaret      ● Bethsaida
(Acco)      Capernaum
Magdala   Sea   ○ Gergesa
Mt. Carmel ▲      Cana   of Galilee
Kishon R.   Nazareth   Tiberias   Hippos

BATANEA

AURANITIS

▲ Mt. Tabor
Nain   R.   ○ Gadara   Abila
Bethany
beyond Jordan

Dor

Caesarea
(Strato's Tower)

Megiddo

Scythopolis ○   ○ Pella

● Dion

DECAPOLIS

SAMARIA

Sebaste   Salim?
(Samaria)
▲ Mt. Ebal   ○ Gerasa
Mt. Gerizim ▲ Sychar   □ Amathus

Me Jarkon      Jordan   Jabbok R.

Antipatris
(Aphek)   Alexandrium

Joppa

PEREA

Philadelphia
○ (Amman)

**(SEMI-INDEPENDENT
MUNICIPALITY)**

Azotus   ● Jamnia   Cyprus □ ● Jericho
(Ashdod)   Emmaus   ▲ Mt. Olivet   □ Esbus (Heshbon)
Jerusalem   Bethany
Bethlehem   □ Hyrcania   ● Medeba

Ashkelon

JUDEA   □ Herodium

Gaza   Hebron
Adora

□ Machaerus

**Dead
Sea**   Arnon R.

Raphia   IDUMEA   Masada □
Arad
Beersheba   □ Malatha

NABATEA

Besor Br.

Zered Br.

0   10   20   30 miles
0   10   20   30 kilometers

## LESSON ONE
# BETTER THAN THE BEST

We all want to be the best in something—whether that means being chosen homecoming queen, most valuable player, employee of the month, or most popular Little League coach. But as we study Christ's teaching, we discover that the world's best is not always God's best. This lesson will contrast the world's goals with God's priorities. You will be challenged to forego seeking the world's best, and instead follow Jesus' perfect example of humble service.

*He has showed you, O man, what is good. And what does the Lord require of you? To act justly and to love mercy and to walk humbly with your God.*
(Micah 6:8)

•••••••••••••••••••••••••••••••••••••••••••••
## JESUS WARNS AGAINST TEMPTATION
*Matthew 18:1-35, Mark 9:33-50, Luke 9:46-50*

*¹At that time the disciples came to Jesus and asked, "Who is the greatest in the kingdom of heaven?"*
*²He called a little child and had him stand among them. ³And he said: "I tell you the truth, unless you change and become like little children, you will never enter the kingdom of heaven. ⁴Therefore, whoever humbles himself like this child is the greatest in the kingdom of heaven.*
*⁵"And whoever welcomes a little child like this in my name welcomes me. ⁶But if anyone causes one of these little ones who believe in me to sin, it would be better for him to have a large millstone*

hung around his neck and to be drowned in the depths of the sea.

⁷"Woe to the world because of the things that cause people to sin! Such things must come, but woe to the man through whom they come! ⁸If your hand or your foot causes you to sin cut it off and throw it away. It is better for you to enter life maimed or crippled than to have two hands or two feet and be thrown into eternal fire. ⁹And if your eye causes you to sin, gouge it out and throw it away. It is better for you to enter life with one eye than to have two eyes and be thrown into the fire of hell.

¹⁰"See that you do not look down on one of these little ones. For I tell you that their angels in heaven always see the face of my Father in heaven.

¹²"What do you think? If a man owns a hundred sheep, and one of them wanders away, will he not leave the ninety-nine on the hills and go to look for the one that wandered off? ¹³And if he finds it, I tell you the truth, he is happier about that one sheep than about the ninety-nine that did not wander off. ¹⁴In the same way your Father in heaven is not willing that any of these little ones should be lost.

¹⁵"If your brother sins against you, go and show him his fault, just between the two of you. If he listens to you, you have won your brother over. ¹⁶But if he will not listen, take one or two others along, so that 'every matter may be established by the testimony of two or three witnesses.' ¹⁷If he refuses to listen to them, tell it to the church; and if he refuses to listen even to the church, treat him as you would a pagan or a tax collector.

¹⁸"I tell you the truth, whatever you bind on earth will be bound in heaven, and whatever you loose on earth will be loosed in heaven.

¹⁹"Again, I tell you that if two of you on earth agree about anything you ask for, it will be done for you by my Father in heaven. ²⁰For where two or three come together in my name, there am I with them."

²¹Then Peter came to Jesus and asked, "Lord, how many times shall I forgive my brother when he

*sins against me? Up to seven times?"*

*²²Jesus answered, "I tell you, not seven times, but seventy-seven times.*

*²³"Therefore, the kingdom of heaven is like a king who wanted to settle accounts with his servants. ²⁴As he began the settlement, a man who owed him ten thousand talents was brought to him. ²⁵Since he was not able to pay, the master ordered that he and his wife and his children and all that he had be sold to repay the debt.*

*²⁶"The servant fell on his knees before him. 'Be patient with me,' he begged, 'and I will pay back everything.' ²⁷The servant's master took pity on him, canceled the debt and let him go.*

*²⁸"But when that servant went out, he found one of his fellow servants who owed him a hundred denarii. He grabbed him and began to choke him. 'Pay back what you owe me!' he demanded.*

*²⁹"His fellow servant fell to his knees and begged him, 'Be patient with me, and I will pay you back.'*

*³⁰"But he refused. Instead, he went off and had the man thrown into prison until he could pay the debt. ³¹When the other servants saw what had happened, they were greatly distressed and went and told their master everything that had happened.*

*³²"Then the master called the servant in. 'You wicked servant,' he said, 'I canceled all that debt of yours because you begged me to. ³³Shouldn't you have had mercy on your fellow servant just as I had on you?' ³⁴In anger his master turned him over to the jailers to be tortured, until he should pay back all he owed.*

*³⁵"This is how my heavenly Father will treat each of you unless you forgive your brother from your heart."* (Matthew 18:1-35)

**Jesus began this teaching on humility** because He had overheard His disciples arguing about who would be greatest in His Kingdom. Instead of vying for position and status, Jesus told the disciples that they would have to humble themselves like children to enter the Kingdom of

God. Childlike humility involves being vulnerable before God, admitting our needs to Him, and believing that He will take care of us.

1. Jesus discussed five major topics in this discourse. Study the passages to identify the major teaching, the illustration Jesus used, and your conclusion about the teaching.

Humility (Matthew 18:1-5)

Sin (Matthew 18:6-10)

God's concern for people (Matthew 18:11-14)

Reconciliation (Matthew 18:15-20)

Forgiveness (Matthew 18:21-35)

2. Why is the "servant of all" called "first" in God's Kingdom?

What have you learned about the Kingdom of God from observing children?

3. Why does Jesus place such great value on children?

4. In what sense do children illustrate the heart condition of those who enter heaven?

What steps could you take to cultivate childlike faith and humility?

5. How do you think the disciples felt when Jesus had a child stand among them as He began to teach?

## JESUS TEACHES ABOUT THE COST OF FOLLOWING HIM *Matthew 8:18-22, 19:1-2; Mark 10:1; Luke 9:51-62; John 7:2-9*

*⁵¹As the time approached for him to be taken up to heaven, Jesus resolutely set out for Jerusalem. ⁵²And he sent messengers on ahead, who went into a Samaritan village to get things ready for him; ⁵³but the people there did not welcome him, because he was heading for Jerusalem. ⁵⁴When the disciples James and John saw this, they asked, "Lord, do you want us to call fire down from heaven to destroy them?" ⁵⁵But Jesus turned and rebuked them, ⁵⁶and they went to another village.*

*⁵⁷As they were walking along the road, a man said to him, "I will follow you wherever you go."*

*⁵⁸Jesus replied, "Foxes have holes and birds of the air have nests, but the Son of Man has no place to lay his head."*

*⁵⁹He said to another man, "Follow me."*

*But the man replied, "Lord, first let me go and bury my father."*

*⁶⁰Jesus said to him, "Let the dead bury their own dead, but you go and proclaim the kingdom of God."*

*⁶¹Still another said, "I will follow you, Lord; but first let me go back and say good-by to my family."*

*⁶²Jesus replied, "No one who puts his hand to the plow and looks back is fit for service in the kingdom of God." (Luke 9:51-62)*

**Jesus never glossed over** the sacrifices involved in being His disciple. He explained that His followers would give up earthly rewards and public recognition, only to gain criticism and persecution. Many people aren't willing to make the sacrifice. Because the world's priorities are still the opposite of Christ's, the cost of following Him hasn't changed. We may have to give up financial security, friends, and even our family relationships to serve in the Kingdom of God.

6. Why did Jesus leave His ministry in Galilee at this time (Luke 9:51; see John 7:1-10)?

7. Jesus said, "No one who puts his hand to the plow and looks back is fit for service in the Kingdom of God." What does He mean by a person who puts his hand to the plow and looks back?

8. Along the way, Jesus laid the claims of discipleship on certain men, all of whom had excuses (Luke 9:57-62). What are some examples today of the three excuses recorded here?

What personal
goals or relation-
ships compete
with your alle-
giance to God?

9. How could an admirable quality like loyalty to one's family and friends be at odds with following Christ?

How can you
begin to loosen
their grip on you,
so that you can
better serve in
God's Kingdom?

10. If a Christian has never sacrificed anything for God, what might this reveal about his or her commitment?

• • • • • • • • • • • • • • • • • • • • • • • • • • • • • • • • • • • • • • • • • •

## JESUS TEACHES OPENLY AT THE TEMPLE
*John 7:10-53*

*¹⁰However, after his brothers had left for the Feast, he went also, not publicly, but in secret. ¹¹Now at the Feast the Jews were watching for him and asking, "Where is that man?"*

*¹²Among the crowds there was widespread whispering about him. Some said, "He is a good man."*

*Others replied, "No, he deceives the people." ¹³But no one would say anything publicly about him for fear of the Jews.*

*¹⁴Not until halfway through the Feast did Jesus go up to the temple courts and begin to teach. ¹⁵The Jews were amazed and asked, "How did this man get such learning without having studied?"*

*¹⁶Jesus answered, "My teaching is not my own. It comes from him who sent me. ¹⁷If anyone chooses to do God's will, he will find out whether my teaching comes from God or whether I speak on my own. ¹⁸He who speaks on his own does so to gain* honor for himself, but he who works for the honor of the one who sent him is a man of truth; there is nothing false about him. ¹⁹Has not Moses given you the law? Yet not one of you keeps the law. Why are you trying to kill me?"

²⁰"You are demon-possessed," the crowd answered. "Who is trying to kill you?"

²¹Jesus said to them, "I did one miracle, and you are all astonished. ²²Yet, because Moses gave you circumcision (though actually it did not come from Moses, but from the patriarchs), you circumcise a child on the Sabbath. ²³Now if a child can be circumcised on the Sabbath so that the law of Moses may not be broken, why are you angry with me for healing the whole man on the Sabbath? ²⁴Stop judging by mere appearances, and make a right judgment."

²⁵At that point some of the people of Jerusalem began to ask, "Isn't this the man they are trying to kill? ²⁶Here he is, speaking publicly, and they are not saying a word to him. Have the authorities really concluded that he is the Christ? ²⁷But we know where this man is from; when the Christ comes, no one will know where he is from."

²⁸Then Jesus, still teaching in the temple courts, cried out, "Yes, you know me, and you know where I am from. I am not here on my own, but he who sent me is true. You do not know him, ²⁹but I know him because I am from him and he sent me."

³⁰At this they tried to seize him, but no one laid a hand on him, because his time had not yet come. ³¹Still, many in the crowd put their faith in him. They said, "When the Christ comes, will he do more miraculous signs than this man?"

³²The Pharisees heard the crowd whispering such things about him. Then the chief priests and the Pharisees sent temple guards to arrest him.

³³Jesus said, "I am with you for only a short time, and then I go to the one who sent me. ³⁴You will look for me, but you will not find me; and where I am, you cannot come."

³⁵The Jews said to one another, "Where does this

man intend to go that we cannot find him? Will he go where our people live scattered among the Greeks, and teach the Greeks? [36]What did he mean when he said, 'You will look for me, but you will not find me,' and 'Where I am, you cannot come'?"

[37]On the last and greatest day of the Feast, Jesus stood and said in a loud voice, "If anyone is thirsty, let him come to me and drink. [38]Whoever believes in me, as the Scripture has said, streams of living water will flow from within him." [39]By this he meant the Spirit, whom those who believed in him were later to receive. Up to that time the Spirit had not been given, since Jesus had not yet been glorified.

[40]On hearing his words, some of the people said, "Surely this man is the Prophet."

[41]Others said, "He is the Christ."

Still others asked, "How can the Christ come from Galilee? [42]Does not the Scripture say that the Christ will come from David's family and from Bethlehem, the town where David lived?" [43]Thus the people were divided because of Jesus. [44]Some wanted to seize him, but no one laid a hand on him.

[45]Finally the temple guards went back to the chief priests and Pharisees, who asked them, "Why didn't you bring him in?"

[46]"No one ever spoke the way this man does," the guards declared.

[47]"You mean he has deceived you also?" the Pharisees retorted. [48]"Has any of the rulers or of the Pharisees believed in him? [49]No! But this mob that knows nothing of the law—there is a curse on them."

[50]Nicodemus, who had gone to Jesus earlier and who was one of their own number, asked, [51]"Does our law condemn anyone without first hearing him to find out what he is doing?"

[52]They replied, "Are you from Galilee, too? Look into it, and you will find that a prophet does not come out of Galilee."

[53]Then each went to his own home. (John 7:10-53)

**The Feast of Tabernacles came in the Jewish month of Tisri**, present-day September/October, and lasted eight days. Jesus was the main topic of conversation at this Jewish celebration. Everyone had a different opinion about who He was, but no one publicly supported Him because they feared retaliation from the Pharisees.

11. What are some of the wrong opinions about Jesus revealed in this incident?

12. How did Jesus respond to the people who had misconceptions about Him?

What conclusions about Jesus do you draw from this passage?

13. Why did Jesus insist that His message was not original, but came from "the Father"?

What worldly goal
do you need to
give up?

14. In light of what they wanted to know and what Jesus said and did, what conclusions about Jesus would those at the Feast of Tabernacles have reached?

15. What does this passage indicate about the power of Jesus' word?

What act of
humble service
could you do this
week in Christ's
name?

**Jesus could have been the most popular teacher in the world!** His power impressed even the strongest skeptics, but His controversial teaching turned away would-be supporters. Jesus' message goes against everything the world tells us is important. Jesus wants us to be humble servants instead of seeking popularity, prestige, and security.

# LESSON TWO
# WITHOUT A DOUBT

✛

Some people think that if they lead good lives, God will welcome them into the Kingdom of Heaven. Others know they'll never make it on their own merit, so they hope to be allowed in because of their parent's or spouse's faith. But Jesus tells us that good works or the beliefs of others won't get anyone into Heaven. This lesson will show what you need to do now to enter the Kingdom of God and enjoy His presence forever.

*"Therefore, my brothers, I want you to know that through Jesus the forgiveness of sins is proclaimed to you. Through him everyone who believes is justified from everything you could not be justified from by the law of Moses."*
(Acts 13:38-39)

••••••••••••••••••••••••••••••••••••••••

## JESUS FORGIVES AN ADULTEROUS WOMAN *John 8:1-11*

*¹But Jesus went to the Mount of Olives. ²At dawn he appeared again in the temple courts, where all the people gathered around him, and he sat down to teach them. ³The teachers of the law and the Pharisees brought in a woman caught in adultery. They made her stand before the group ⁴and said to Jesus, "Teacher, this woman was caught in the act of adultery. ⁵In the Law Moses commanded us to stone such women. Now what do you say?" ⁶They were using this question as a trap, in order to have a basis for accusing him.*

*But Jesus bent down and started to write on the ground with his finger. ⁷When they kept on questioning him, he straightened up and said to them, "If any one of you is without sin, let him be the first to throw a stone at her." ⁸Again he stooped down and wrote on the ground.*

⁹*At this, those who heard began to go away one at a time, the older ones first, until only Jesus was left, with the woman still standing there. ¹⁰Jesus straightened up and asked her, "Woman, where are they? Has no one condemned you?"*

¹¹*"No one, sir," she said.*

*"Then neither do I condemn you," Jesus declared. "Go now and leave your life of sin."*
(John 8:1-11)

**The Pharisees couldn't put up with Jesus any longer!** They devised a "fool-proof" plan to trap Him. They brought before Him a woman caught in the act of adultery, knowing full well that Old Testament law said any person caught in that sin should be stoned to death. If Jesus told them to execute her, the Pharisees could turn him over to the Romans, who did not permit their subjects to carry out death sentences. If he tried to excuse her actions, the religious leaders could denounce Him. To their amazement, Jesus came up with the perfect solution to the dilemma. At the same time, He taught them a lesson about humility and forgiveness.

In light of this passage, how do you need to adjust your attitude toward people whose sins have been exposed?

1. How did Jesus defeat the Pharisees' plot?

2. How did Jesus treat this woman who, according to Old Testament law, deserved death?

3. How do we typically treat people who are known sinners like the woman in this passage?

If you have been unforgiving toward a friend, what first step can you take today toward reconciliation?

4. How can we imitate Christ's example when we interact with others?

••••••••••••••••••••••••••••••••••••••••••••••••

## JESUS TEACHES ABOUT HIMSELF
### John 8:12-59

*¹²When Jesus spoke again to the people, he said, "I am the light of the world. Whoever follows me will never walk in darkness, but will have the light of life."*

*¹³The Pharisees challenged him, "Here you are, appearing as your own witness; your testimony is not valid."*

*¹⁴Jesus answered, "Even if I testify on my own behalf, my testimony is valid, for I know where I came from and where I am going. But you have no idea where I come from or where I am going. ¹⁵You judge by human standards; I pass judgment on no one. ¹⁶But if I do judge, my decisions are right, because I am not alone. I stand with the Father, who sent me. ¹⁷In your own Law it is written that the testimony of two men is valid. ¹⁸I am one who testifies for myself; my other witness is the Father, who sent me."*

*¹⁹Then they asked him, "Where is your father?"*

*"You do not know me or my Father," Jesus replied. "If you knew me, you would know my Father also." ²⁰He spoke these words while teaching*

in the temple area near the place where the offerings were put. Yet no one seized him, because his time had not yet come.

²¹Once more Jesus said to them, "I am going away, and you will look for me, and you will die in your sin. Where I go, you cannot come."

²²This made the Jews ask, "Will he kill himself? Is that why he says, 'Where I go, you cannot come'?"

²³But he continued, "You are from below; I am from above. You are of this world; I am not of this world. ²⁴I told you that you would die in your sins; if you do not believe that I am the one I claim to be, you will indeed die in your sins."

²⁵"Who are you?" they asked.

"Just what I have been claiming all along," Jesus replied. ²⁶"I have much to say in judgment of you. But he who sent me is reliable, and what I have heard from him I tell the world."

²⁷They did not understand that he was telling them about his Father. ²⁸So Jesus said, "When you have lifted up the Son of Man, then you will know that I am the one I claim to be and that I do nothing on my own but speak just what the Father has taught me. ²⁹The one who sent me is with me; he has not left me alone, for I always do what pleases him." ³⁰Even as he spoke, many put their faith in him.

³¹To the Jews who had believed him, Jesus said, "If you hold to my teaching, you are really my disciples. ³²Then you will know the truth, and the truth will set you free."

³³They answered him, "We are Abraham's descendants and have never been slaves of anyone. How can you say that we shall be set free?"

³⁴Jesus replied, "I tell you the truth, everyone who sins is a slave to sin. ³⁵Now a slave has no permanent place in the family, but a son belongs to it forever. ³⁶So if the Son sets you free, you will be free indeed. ³⁷I know you are Abraham's descendants. Yet you are ready to kill me, because you have no room for my word. ³⁸I am telling you what I have seen in the Father's presence, and you do what you

have heard from your father."

³⁹"Abraham is our father," they answered.

"If you were Abraham's children," said Jesus, "then you would do the things Abraham did. ⁴⁰As it is, you are determined to kill me, a man who has told you the truth that I heard from God. Abraham did not do such things. ⁴¹You are doing the things your own father does."

"We are not illegitimate children," they protested. "The only Father we have is God himself."

⁴²Jesus said to them, "If God were your Father, you would love me, for I came from God and now am here. I have not come on my own; but he sent me. ⁴³Why is my language not clear to you? Because you are unable to hear what I say. ⁴⁴You belong to your father, the devil, and you want to carry out your father's desire. He was a murderer from the beginning, not holding to the truth, for there is no truth in him. When he lies, he speaks his native language, for he is a liar and the father of lies. ⁴⁵Yet because I tell the truth, you do not believe me! ⁴⁶Can any of you prove me guilty of sin? If I am telling the truth, why don't you believe me? ⁴⁷He who belongs to God hears what God says. The reason you do not hear is that you do not belong to God."

⁴⁸The Jews answered him, "Aren't we right in saying that you are a Samaritan and demon-possessed?"

⁴⁹"I am not possessed by a demon," said Jesus, "but I honor my Father and you dishonor me. ⁵⁰I am not seeking glory for myself; but there is one who seeks it, and he is the judge. ⁵¹I tell you the truth, if anyone keeps my word, he will never see death."

⁵²At this the Jews exclaimed, "Now we know that you are demon-possessed! Abraham died and so did the prophets, yet you say that if anyone keeps your word, he will never taste death. ⁵³Are you greater than our father Abraham? He died, and so did the prophets. Who do you think you are?"

⁵⁴Jesus replied, "If I glorify myself, my glory means nothing. My Father, whom you claim as

*your God, is the one who glorifies me. ⁵⁵Though you
do not know him, I know him. If I said I did not, I
would be a liar like you, but I do know him and
keep his word. ⁵⁶Your father Abraham rejoiced at the
thought of seeing my day; he saw it and was glad."*

*⁵⁷"You are not yet fifty years old," the Jews said
to him, "and you have seen Abraham!"*

*⁵⁸"I tell you the truth," Jesus answered, "before
Abraham was born, I am!" ⁵⁹At this, they picked up
stones to stone him, but Jesus hid himself, slipping
away from the temple grounds.* (John 8:12-59)

**Using the preceding incident as a starting
point,** Jesus began to explain to the crowd who
He was and on whose authority He acted. The
religious leaders continually challenged His
authority—they said His testimony wasn't
legally valid because He served as His own witness. Old Testament law required the testimony
of at least two witnesses to prove a case
(Deuteronomy 19:15). The Pharisees didn't real-
ize that Jesus' own testimony, supported by the
Father's, fulfilled the number required by law.

5. List all statements in this passage where
Jesus used the phrase "I am" about Himself,
identifying the context and meaning of each
statement.

6. Why did Jesus place such an emphasis on His origin and destination ("where I came from and where I am going")?

What have you learned about Jesus from this passage?

7. What conclusions did the Jews draw from these statements?

8. According to Jesus, what will happen to those who don't believe He is the Son of God?

How does your understanding of who Jesus is affect your daily life?

• • • • • • • • • • • • • • • • • • • • • • • • • • • • • • • • • • •

## JESUS HEALS A BLIND MAN
*John 9:1-41*

*¹As he went along, he saw a man blind from birth. ²His disciples asked him, "Rabbi, who sinned, this man or his parents, that he was born blind?"*

*³"Neither this man nor his parents sinned," said Jesus, "but this happened so that the work of*

God might be displayed in his life. ⁴As long as it is day, we must do the work of him who sent me. Night is coming, when no one can work. ⁵While I am in the world, I am the light of the world."

⁶Having said this, he spit on the ground, made some mud with the saliva, and put it on the man's eyes. ⁷"Go," he told him, "wash in the Pool of Siloam" (this word means Sent). So the man went and washed, and came home seeing.

⁸His neighbors and those who had formerly seen him begging asked, "Isn't this the same man who used to sit and beg?" ⁹Some claimed that he was.

Others said, "No, he only looks like him."

But he himself insisted, "I am the man."

¹⁰"How then were your eyes opened?" they demanded.

¹¹He replied, "The man they call Jesus made some mud and put it on my eyes. He told me to go to Siloam and wash. So I went and washed, and then I could see."

¹²"Where is this man?" they asked him.

"I don't know," he said.

¹³They brought to the Pharisees the man who had been blind. ¹⁴Now the day on which Jesus had made the mud and opened the man's eyes was a Sabbath. ¹⁵Therefore the Pharisees also asked him how he had received his sight. "He put mud on my eyes," the man replied, "and I washed, and now I see."

¹⁶Some of the Pharisees said, "This man is not from God, for he does not keep the Sabbath."

But others asked, "How can a sinner do such miraculous signs?" So they were divided.

¹⁷Finally they turned again to the blind man, "What have you to say about him? It was your eyes he opened."

The man replied, "He is a prophet."

¹⁸The Jews still did not believe that he had been blind and had received his sight until they sent for the man's parents. ¹⁹"Is this your son?" they asked. "Is this the one you say was born

blind? How is it that now he can see?"

²⁰"We know he is our son," the parents answered, "and we know he was born blind. ²¹But how he can see now, or who opened his eyes, we don't know. Ask him. He is of age; he will speak for himself." ²²His parents said this because they were afraid of the Jews, for already the Jews had decided that anyone who acknowledged that Jesus was the Christ would be put out of the synagogue. ²³That was why his parents said, "He is of age; ask him."

²⁴A second time they summoned the man who had been blind. "Give glory to God," they said. "We know this man is a sinner."

²⁵He replied, "Whether he is a sinner or not, I don't know. One thing I do know. I was blind but now I see!"

²⁶Then they asked him, "What did he do to you? How did he open your eyes?"

²⁷He answered, "I have told you already and you did not listen. Why do you want to hear it again? Do you want to become his disciples, too?"

²⁸Then they hurled insults at him and said, "You are this fellow's disciple! We are disciples of Moses! ²⁹We know that God spoke to Moses, but as for this fellow, we don't even know where he comes from."

³⁰The man answered, "Now that is remarkable! You don't know where he comes from, yet he opened my eyes. ³¹We know that God does not listen to sinners. He listens to the godly man who does his will. ³²Nobody has ever heard of opening the eyes of a man born blind. ³³If this man were not from God, he could do nothing."

³⁴To this they replied, "You were steeped in sin at birth; how dare you lecture us!" And they threw him out.

³⁵Jesus heard that they had thrown him out, and when he found him, he said, "Do you believe in the Son of Man?"

³⁶"Who is he, sir?" the man asked. "Tell me so that I may believe in him."

³⁷Jesus said, "You have now seen him; in fact,

*he is the one speaking with you."*

*<sup>38</sup>Then the man said, "Lord, I believe," and he worshiped him.*

*<sup>39</sup>Jesus said, "For judgment I have come into this world, so that the blind will see and those who see will become blind."*

*<sup>40</sup>Some Pharisees who were with him heard him say this and asked, "What? Are we blind too?"*

*<sup>41</sup>Jesus said, "If you were blind, you would not be guilty of sin; but now that you claim you can see, your guilt remains."* (John 9:1-41)

**After pointing out the spiritual blindness of the Jews** when they did not recognize Him as the Light of the World, Jesus demonstrated His power by bringing light to a man blind since birth. The man's life was miraculously changed because of Jesus' power and compassion. He put his faith in Jesus and told everyone he met of his new life in Christ.

9. What problem was posed by the disciples' question (John 9:2)?

10. How did Jesus resolve the problem?

11. What kind of blindness did Jesus see in the Pharisees?

What steps can you take this week to sharpen your spiritual understanding?

12. For what reason did Jesus say He came into the world?

13. What impairs our spiritual vision?

What do you plan to do the next time you have doubts about where you will spend eternity?

**"You're not good enough."** "God would never accept someone like you." "You've messed up too many times." Satan tells us all kinds of lies to make us wonder whether we'll make it to Heaven. But our place in Heaven is secure, not because of how hard we try to measure up to God's standards, but because of what Christ has done for us. He gave up His life to overcome the power of sin—all we have to do is believe in Him.

How can you thank God today for the gift of eternal life?

# LESSON THREE
# TENDER LOVING CARE

You can't give away something you don't have. Only those of us who have personally seen and experienced Christ's love can share it with others. Jesus pours His love into us so that it will overflow as we minister to needy people. This lesson will help you recognize the many ways Christ cares for you and will motivate you to share His love with others.

## JESUS IS THE GOOD SHEPHERD
*John 10:1-21*

¹*"I tell you the truth, the man who does not enter the sheep pen by the gate, but climbs in by some other way, is a thief and a robber. ²The man who enters by the gate is the shepherd of his sheep. ³The watchman opens the gate for him, and the sheep listen to his voice. He calls his own sheep by name and leads them out. ⁴When he has brought out all his own, he goes on ahead of them, and his sheep follow him because they know his voice. ⁵But they will never follow a stranger; in fact, they will run away from him because they do not recognize a stranger's voice." ⁶Jesus used this figure of speech, but they did not understand what he was telling them.*

*"I myself will tend my sheep and have them lie down, declares the Sovereign LORD. I will search for the lost and bring back the strays. I will bind up the injured and strengthen the weak, but the sleek and the strong I will destroy. I will shepherd the flock with justice."*
(Ezekiel 34:15-16)

⁷Therefore Jesus said again, "I tell you the truth, I am the gate for the sheep. ⁸All who ever came before me were thieves and robbers, but the sheep did not listen to them. ⁹I am the gate; whoever enters through me will be saved. He will come in and go out, and find pasture. ¹⁰The thief comes only to steal and kill and destroy; I have come that they may have life, and have it to the full.

¹¹"I am the good shepherd. The good shepherd lays down his life for the sheep. ¹²The hired hand is not the shepherd who owns the sheep. So when he sees the wolf coming, he abandons the sheep and runs away. Then the wolf attacks the flock and scatters it. ¹³The man runs away because he is a hired hand and cares nothing for the sheep.

¹⁴"I am the good shepherd; I know my sheep and my sheep know me—¹⁵just as the Father knows me and I know the Father—and I lay down my life for the sheep. ¹⁶I have other sheep that are not of this sheep pen. I must bring them also. They too will listen to my voice, and there shall be one flock and one shepherd. ¹⁷The reason my Father loves me is that I lay down my life—only to take it up again. ¹⁸No one takes it from me, but I lay it down of my own accord. I have authority to lay it down and authority to take it up again. This command I received from my Father."

¹⁹At these words the Jews were again divided. ²⁰Many of them said, "He is demon-possessed and raving mad. Why listen to him?"

²¹But others said, "These are not the sayings of a man possessed by a demon. Can a demon open the eyes of the blind?" (John 10:1-21)

**Jesus continued to reveal more of Himself and His character** through figures of speech, such as the Good Shepherd and the Door. All God's people make one flock and are guided by the same Shepherd, Jesus Christ. He sacrificed His own life to save us from the consequences of sin.

1. What do the various elements represent in this discourse: the sheep, the sheep pen, the gate, the thieves and robbers, the pasture?

2. How is the Good Shepherd different from bad shepherds?

How has Jesus protected and cared for you?

3. How did Jesus' listeners respond to this illustration?

In what ways would you like your relationship with Jesus to be different?

4. What kind of relationship does Jesus want to have with us, according to this passage?

What steps could you take this week to develop a deeper intimacy with Christ?

5. What does this passage teach us about the character of Christ?

•••••••••••••••••••••••••••••••••••••••••••••••••

## JESUS SENDS OUT SEVENTY-TWO MESSENGERS *Luke 10:1-24*

*¹After this the Lord appointed seventy-two others and sent them two by two ahead of him to every town and place where he was about to go. ²He told them, "The harvest is plentiful, but the workers are few. Ask the Lord of the harvest, therefore, to send out workers into his harvest field. ³Go! I am sending you out like lambs among wolves. ⁴Do not take a purse or bag or sandals; and do not greet anyone on the road.*

*⁵"When you enter a house, first say, 'Peace to this house.' ⁶If a man of peace is there, your peace will rest on him; if not, it will return to you. ⁷Stay in that house, eating and drinking whatever they give you, for the worker deserves his wages. Do not move around from house to house.*

*⁸"When you enter a town and are welcomed, eat what is set before you. ⁹Heal the sick who are* there and tell them, 'The kingdom of God is near you.' [10]But when you enter a town and are not welcomed, go into its streets and say, [11]'Even the dust of your town that sticks to our feet we wipe off against you. Yet be sure of this: The kingdom of God is near.' [12]I tell you, it will be more bearable on that day for Sodom than for that town.

[13]"Woe to you, Korazin! Woe to you, Bethsaida! For if the miracles that were performed in you had been performed in Tyre and Sidon, they would have repented long ago, sitting in sackcloth and ashes. [14]But it will be more bearable for Tyre and Sidon at the judgment than for you. [15]And you, Capernaum, will you be lifted up to the skies? No, you will go down to the depths.

[16]"He who listens to you listens to me; he who rejects you rejects me; but he who rejects me rejects him who sent me."

[17]The seventy-two returned with joy and said, "Lord, even the demons submit to us in your name."

[18]He replied, "I saw Satan fall like lightning from heaven. [19]I have given you authority to trample on snakes and scorpions and to overcome all the power of the enemy; nothing will harm you. [20]However, do not rejoice that the spirits submit to you, but rejoice that your names are written in heaven."

[21]At that time Jesus, full of joy through the Holy Spirit, said, "I praise you, Father, Lord of heaven and earth, because you have hidden these things from the wise and learned, and revealed them to little children. Yes, Father, for this was your good pleasure.

[2]"All things have been committed to me by my Father. No one knows who the Son is except the Father, and no one knows who the Father is except the Son and those to whom the Son chooses to reveal him."

[23]Then he turned to his disciples and said privately, "Blessed are the eyes that see what you see. [24]For I tell you that many prophets and kings wanted to see what you see but did not see it, and to hear what you hear but did not hear it." (Luke 10:1-24)

**What an overwhelming task!** Jesus sent thirty-six teams of two ahead of Him to prepare the multitudes of people He planned to visit. But before the workers left, He told them that prayer would be the key to their success. If you feel helpless to do what God has asked of you, tap into God's unlimited power through prayer. He promises to work through you, if you will depend on Him.

6. What was the mission of the disciples, and how did Jesus equip them for their task?

What can you do the next time you feel discouraged about the responsibilities God has given you?

7. When the workers returned to Jesus, how did He help them refocus their priorities?

8. How do we typically evaluate the effectiveness of a ministry?

9. How can our accomplishments distract us
   from what God thinks is most important?

● ● ● ● ● ● ● ● ● ● ● ● ● ● ● ● ● ● ● ● ● ● ● ● ● ● ● ● ● ● ● ● ● ● ● ● ● ● ● ● ● ● ● ● ● ● ● ●

## JESUS TELLS THE PARABLE OF THE GOOD
## SAMARITAN *Luke 10:25-37*

*²⁵On one occasion an expert in the law stood up to
test Jesus. "Teacher," he asked, "what must I do to
inherit eternal life?"*

*²⁶"What is written in the Law?" he replied.
"How do you read it?"*

*²⁷He answered: "'Love the Lord your God with
all your heart and with all your soul and with all
your strength and with all your mind'; and, 'Love
your neighbor as yourself.'"*

*²⁸"You have answered correctly," Jesus replied.
"Do this and you will live."*

*²⁹But he wanted to justify himself, so he asked
Jesus, "And who is my neighbor?"*

*³⁰In reply Jesus said: "A man was going down
from Jerusalem to Jericho, when he fell into the
hands of robbers. They stripped him of his clothes,
beat him and went away, leaving him half dead. ³¹A
priest happened to be going down the same road,
and when he saw the man, he passed by on the
other side. ³²So too, a Levite, when he came to the
place and saw him, passed by on the other side.
³³But a Samaritan, as he traveled, came where the
man was; and when he saw him, he took pity on
him. ³⁴He went to him and bandaged his wounds,
pouring on oil and wine. Then he put the man on
his own donkey, took him to an inn and took care*

*of him. ³⁵The next day he took out two silver coins and gave them to the innkeeper. 'Look after him,' he said, 'and when I return, I will reimburse you for any extra expense you may have.'*

*³⁶"Which of these three do you think was a neighbor to the man who fell into the hands of robbers?"*

*³⁷The expert in the law replied, "The one who had mercy on him."*

*Jesus told him, "Go and do likewise."* (Luke 10:25-37)

**When a legal expert asked Jesus** how he could gain eternal life, Jesus told him to put into practice the principles of the law. He illustrated His point by telling one of His best known stories. In the parable of the good Samaritan, Jesus clearly reveals what kinds of attitudes and actions are pleasing to God.

10. How did the legal expert sum up the requirements of the Law?

What specific changes do you need to make in your attitude toward the needy people around you?

11. What attitudes did the different people in the story display toward the injured man?

12. What important principles about loving our neighbors can we learn from this story?

To whom do you need to demonstrate Christlike compassion and love?

13. What excuses do we use to neglect the needs of others?

••••••••••••••••••••••••••••••••••••••••••••••••

## JESUS VISITS MARY AND MARTHA
*Luke 10:38-42*

*[38]As Jesus and his disciples were on their way, he came to a village where a woman named Martha opened her home to him. [39]She had a sister called Mary, who sat at the Lord's feet listening to what he said. [40]But Martha was distracted by all the preparations that had to be made. She came to him and asked, "Lord, don't you care that my sister has left me to do the work by myself? Tell her to help me!"*

*[41]"Martha, Martha," the Lord answered, "you are worried and upset about many things, [42]but only one thing is needed. Mary has chosen what is better, and it will not be taken away from her."*
(Luke 10:38-42)

**While the story of the good Samaritan** emphasizes the importance of good deeds, Jesus' visit to the home of Mary and Martha shows the importance of meditation and time with Him. Both women loved Jesus, but had different ways of showing their devotion.

Are your priorities more like Mary's or Martha's?

14. What were some of the differences between Mary and Martha?

How can you find the right balance between worship and service?

15. Why do you think Mary's service was more pleasing to Jesus than Martha's?

How have you recently experienced Jesus' love?

16. What do we learn from this passage about the priorities Christ wants us to have?

In what tangible way could you demonstrate Christlike love to someone this week?

**The needs of the world can be overwhelming.** Instead of throwing your hands up in despair, follow Christ's perfect example. Like a good shepherd, He lovingly cares for you and faithfully meets all of your needs. Share His compassion and love with the needy people around you. But as you serve others, continually check your priorities. Don't allow your service to interfere with your worship of Christ.

# SHARPER VISION

It's hard to believe that religious leaders could be so blind to the truth! But when Jesus revealed Himself as the Messiah, the Pharisees didn't recognize Him. Even though we have the complete story of Jesus' life and ministry, our understanding of the truth can also be clouded. This lesson will give us a better understanding of Christ's teaching about Himself and His Kingdom.

*We know also that the Son of God has come and has given us understanding, so that we may know him who is true. And we are in him who is true — even in his Son Jesus Christ. He is the true God and eternal life.*
(1 John 5:20)

## JESUS TEACHES HIS DISCIPLES ABOUT PRAYER *Matthew 6:9-15, Luke 11:1-13*

*¹One day Jesus was praying in a certain place. When he finished, one of his disciples said to him, "Lord, teach us to pray, just as John taught his disciples."*

*²He said to them, "When you pray, say:*

*"'Father,*
*hallowed be your name,*
*your kingdom come.*
*³Give us each day our daily bread.*
*⁴Forgive us our sins,*
*for we also forgive everyone who sins against us.*
*And lead us not into temptation.'"*

*⁵Then he said to them, "Suppose one of you has a friend, and he goes to him at midnight and says, 'Friend, lend me three loaves of bread, ⁶because a friend of mine on a journey has come to me, and I have nothing to set before him.'*

*⁷"Then the one inside answers, 'Don't bother me. The door is already locked, and my children are with me in bed. I can't get up and give you anything.' ⁸I tell you, though he will not get up and give him the bread because he is his friend, yet because of the man's boldness he will get up and give him as much as he needs.*

*⁹"So I say to you: Ask and it will be given to you; seek and you will find; knock and the door will be opened to you. ¹⁰For everyone who asks receives; he who seeks finds; and to him who knocks, the door will be opened.*

*¹¹"Which of you fathers, if your son asks for a fish, will give him a snake instead? ¹²Or if he asks for an egg, will give him a scorpion? ¹³If you then, though you are evil, know how to give good gifts to your children, how much more will your Father in heaven give the Holy Spirit to those who ask him!"* (Luke 11:1-13)

**Even though He was the Son the God,** Jesus prayed regularly. His disciples knew their need for this relationship with the Father, so they asked Him to teach them. In response, Jesus emphasized the importance of praising God, forgiving others, and practicing persistence in prayer. If Jesus prioritized prayer in His life, how much *more* do we need to spend time with God in this way?

1. According to this passage, what attitudes should characterize our prayers?

2. What should we remember about God's character when we pray?

3. Why did Jesus make prayer a priority in His own life?

4. How do you think persevering in prayer affects a person's heart and attitudes?

How can you strengthen your personal prayer life?

5. Why do we tend to give up praying so easily?

## JESUS EXPOSES THE RELIGIOUS LEADERS
*Luke 11:37–12:12*

³⁷When Jesus had finished speaking, a Pharisee invited him to eat with him; so he went in and reclined at the table. ³⁸But the Pharisee, noticing that Jesus did not first wash before the meal, was surprised.

³⁹Then the Lord said to him, "Now then, you Pharisees clean the outside of the cup and dish, but inside you are full of greed and wickedness. ⁴⁰You foolish people! Did not the one who made the outside make the inside also? ⁴¹But give what is inside the dish to the poor, and everything will be clean for you.

⁴²"Woe to you Pharisees, because you give God a tenth of your mint, rue and all other kinds of garden herbs, but you neglect justice and the love of God. You should have practiced the latter without leaving the former undone.

⁴³"Woe to you Pharisees, because you love the most important seats in the synagogues and greetings in the marketplaces.

⁴⁴"Woe to you, because you are like unmarked graves, which men walk over without knowing it."

⁴⁵One of the experts in the law answered him, "Teacher, when you say these things, you insult us also."

⁴⁶Jesus replied, "And you experts in the law, woe to you, because you load people down with burdens they can hardly carry, and you yourselves will not lift one finger to help them.

⁴⁷"Woe to you, because you build tombs for the prophets, and it was your forefathers who killed them. ⁴⁸So you testify that you approve of what your forefathers did; they killed the prophets, and you build their tombs. ⁴⁹Because of this, God in his wisdom said, 'I will send them prophets and apostles, some of whom they will kill and others they will persecute.' ⁵⁰Therefore this generation will be held responsible for the blood of all the prophets that has been shed since the beginning of the world, ⁵¹from the blood of Abel to the blood of Zechariah,

who was killed between the altar and the sanctuary. Yes, I tell you, this generation will be held responsible for it all.

⁵²"Woe to you experts in the law, because you have taken away the key to knowledge. You yourselves have not entered, and you have hindered those who were entering."

⁵³When Jesus left there, the Pharisees and the teachers of the law began to oppose him fiercely and to besiege him with questions, ⁵⁴waiting to catch him in something he might say.

¹Meanwhile, when a crowd of many thousands had gathered, so that they were trampling on one another, Jesus began to speak first to his disciples, saying: "Be on your guard against the yeast of the Pharisees, which is hypocrisy. ²There is nothing concealed that will not be disclosed, or hidden that will not be made known. ³What you have said in the dark will be heard in the daylight, and what you have whispered in the ear in the inner rooms will be proclaimed from the roofs.

⁴"I tell you, my friends, do not be afraid of those who kill the body and after that can do no more. ⁵But I will show you whom you should fear: Fear him who, after the killing of the body, has power to throw you into hell. Yes, I tell you, fear him. ⁶Are not five sparrows sold for two pennies? Yet not one of them is forgotten by God. ⁷Indeed, the very hairs of your head are all numbered. Don't be afraid; you are worth more than many sparrows.

⁸"I tell you, whoever acknowledges me before men, the Son of Man will also acknowledge him before the angels of God. ⁹But he who disowns me before men will be disowned before the angels of God. ¹⁰And everyone who speaks a word against the Son of Man will be forgiven, but anyone who blasphemes against the Holy Spirit will not be forgiven.

¹¹"When you are brought before synagogues, rulers and authorities, do not worry about how you will defend yourselves or what you will say, ¹²for the Holy Spirit will teach you at that time what you should say." (Luke 11:37–12:12)

**While the Pharisees appeared to be "clean"** because of their strict obedience to the Law, Jesus exposed the rottenness in their hearts. They had taken the practice of ceremonial washing, which originally applied primarily to priests, and demanded that everyone follow it. Jesus knew that, despite their actions, their hearts were far away from God. Clearly, God cares more about the condition of our hearts than our reputations, outward appearance, or accomplishments.

6. Why was Jesus so hard on the Pharisees?

7. Why are promoting justice and giving to the poor so central to a truly spiritual life?

8. How might we hinder others from coming to God by what we do and what we omit doing?

9. In what ways do we try to change people on the outside rather than helping them develop inner character?

How can we determine whether we are evaluating ourselves according to God's standards or the world's standards?

10. Why do we focus so much on how we look, what we accomplish, and what people think of us?

What steps could you take this week to develop your inner character?

. . . . . . . . . . . . . . . . . . . . . . . . . . . . . . . . . . . . . . . . . . . .

## JESUS WARNS THE PEOPLE
*Luke 12:13–13:21*

*[13]Someone in the crowd said to him, "Teacher, tell my brother to divide the inheritance with me."*

*[14]Jesus replied, "Man, who appointed me a judge or an arbiter between you?" [15]Then he said to them, "Watch out! Be on your guard against all kinds of greed; a man's life does not consist in the abundance of his possessions."*

*[16]And he told them this parable: "The ground of*

49

a certain rich man produced a good crop. <sup>17</sup>He thought to himself, 'What shall I do? I have no place to store my crops.'

<sup>18</sup>"Then he said, 'This is what I'll do. I will tear down my barns and build bigger ones, and there I will store all my grain and my goods. <sup>19</sup>And I'll say to myself, "You have plenty of good things laid up for many years. Take life easy; eat, drink and be merry."'

<sup>20</sup>"But God said to him, 'You fool! This very night your life will be demanded from you. Then who will get what you have prepared for yourself?'

<sup>21</sup>"This is how it will be with anyone who stores up things for himself but is not rich toward God."

<sup>22</sup>Then Jesus said to his disciples: "Therefore I tell you, do not worry about your life, what you will eat; or about your body, what you will wear. <sup>23</sup>Life is more than food, and the body more than clothes. <sup>24</sup>Consider the ravens: They do not sow or reap, they have no storeroom or barn; yet God feeds them. And how much more valuable you are than birds! <sup>25</sup>Who of you by worrying can add a single hour to his life? <sup>26</sup>Since you cannot do this very little thing, why do you worry about the rest?

<sup>27</sup>"Consider how the lilies grow. They do not labor or spin. Yet I tell you, not even Solomon in all his splendor was dressed like one of these. <sup>28</sup>If that is how God clothes the grass of the field, which is here today, and tomorrow is thrown into the fire, how much more will he clothe you, O you of little faith! <sup>29</sup>And do not set your heart on what you will eat or drink; do not worry about it. <sup>30</sup>For the pagan world runs after all such things, and your Father knows that you need them. <sup>31</sup>But seek his kingdom, and these things will be given to you as well.

<sup>32</sup>"Do not be afraid, little flock, for your Father has been pleased to give you the kingdom. <sup>33</sup>Sell your possessions and give to the poor. Provide purses for yourselves that will not wear out, a treasure in heaven that will not be exhausted, where no thief comes near and no moth destroys. <sup>34</sup>For where

*your treasure is, there your heart will be also.*

³⁵*"Be dressed ready for service and keep your lamps burning, ³⁶like men waiting for their master to return from a wedding banquet, so that when he comes and knocks they can immediately open the door for him. ³⁷It will be good for those servants whose master finds them watching when he comes. I tell you the truth, he will dress himself to serve, will have them recline at the table and will come and wait on them. ³⁸It will be good for those servants whose master finds them ready, even if he comes in the second or third watch of the night. ³⁹But understand this: If the owner of the house had known at what hour the thief was coming, he would not have let his house be broken into. ⁴⁰You also must be ready, because the Son of Man will come at an hour when you do not expect him."*

⁴¹*Peter asked, "Lord, are you telling this parable to us, or to everyone?"*

⁴²*The Lord answered, "Who then is the faithful and wise manager, whom the master puts in charge of his servants to give them their food allowance at the proper time? ⁴³It will be good for that servant whom the master finds doing so when he returns. ⁴⁴I tell you the truth, he will put him in charge of all his possessions. ⁴⁵But suppose the servant says to himself, 'My master is taking a long time in coming,' and he then begins to beat the menservants and maidservants and to eat and drink and get drunk. ⁴⁶The master of that servant will come on a day when he does not expect him and at an hour he is not aware of. He will cut him to pieces and assign him a place with the unbelievers.*

⁴⁷*"That servant who knows his master's will and does not get ready or does not do what his master wants will be beaten with many blows. ⁴⁸But the one who does not know and does things deserving punishment will be beaten with few blows. From everyone who has been given much, much will be demanded; and from the one who has been entrusted with much, much more will be asked.*

⁴⁹*"I have come to bring fire on the earth, and*

how I wish it were already kindled! ⁵⁰But I have a baptism to undergo, and how distressed I am until it is completed! ⁵¹Do you think I came to bring peace on earth? No, I tell you, but division. ⁵²From now on there will be five in one family divided against each other, three against two and two against three. ⁵³They will be divided, father against son and son against father, mother against daughter and daughter against mother, mother-in-law against daughter-in-law and daughter-in-law against mother-in-law."

⁵⁴He said to the crowd: "When you see a cloud rising in the west, immediately you say, 'It's going to rain,' and it does. ⁵⁵And when the south wind blows, you say, 'It's going to be hot,' and it is. ⁵⁶Hypocrites! You know how to interpret the appearance of the earth and the sky. How is it that you don't know how to interpret this present time?

⁵⁷"Why don't you judge for yourselves what is right? ⁵⁸As you are going with your adversary to the magistrate, try hard to be reconciled to him on the way, or he may drag you off to the judge, and the judge turn you over to the officer, and the officer throw you into prison. ⁵⁹I tell you, you will not get out until you have paid the last penny."

¹Now there were some present at that time who told Jesus about the Galileans whose blood Pilate had mixed with their sacrifices. ²Jesus answered, "Do you think that these Galileans were worse sinners than all the other Galileans because they suffered this way? ³I tell you, no! But unless you repent, you too will all perish. ⁴Or those eighteen who died when the tower in Siloam fell on them— do you think they were more guilty than all the others living in Jerusalem? ⁵I tell you, no! But unless you repent, you too will all perish."

⁶Then he told this parable: "A man had a fig tree, planted in his vineyard, and he went to look for fruit on it, but did not find any. ⁷So he said to the man who took care of the vineyard, 'For three years now I've been coming to look for fruit on this fig tree and haven't found any. Cut it down!

Why should it use up the soil?'

⁸ "'Sir,' the man replied, 'leave it alone for one more year, and I'll dig around it and fertilize it. ⁹If it bears fruit next year, fine! If not, then cut it down.'"

¹⁰On a Sabbath Jesus was teaching in one of the synagogues, ¹¹and a woman was there who had been crippled by a spirit for eighteen years. She was bent over and could not straighten up at all. ¹²When Jesus saw her, he called her forward and said to her, "Woman, you are set free from your infirmity." ¹³Then he put his hands on her, and immediately she straightened up and praised God.

¹⁴Indignant because Jesus had healed on the Sabbath, the synagogue ruler said to the people, "There are six days for work. So come and be healed on those days, not on the Sabbath."

¹⁵The Lord answered him, "You hypocrites! Doesn't each of you on the Sabbath untie his ox or donkey from the stall and lead it out to give it water? ¹⁶Then should not this woman, a daughter of Abraham, whom Satan has kept bound for eighteen long years, be set free on the Sabbath day from what bound her?"

¹⁷When he said this, all his opponents were humiliated, but the people were delighted with all the wonderful things he was doing.

¹⁸Then Jesus asked, "What is the kingdom of God like? What shall I compare it to? ¹⁹It is like a mustard seed, which a man took and planted in his garden. It grew and became a tree, and the birds of the air perched in its branches."

²⁰Again he asked, "What shall I compare the kingdom of God to? ²¹It is like yeast that a woman took and mixed into a large amount of flour until it worked all through the dough." (Luke 12:13–13:21)

**Fear of what people think** can drag a person away from following Jesus boldly. Other obstacles include materialism, worry, and love of comfort and security.

11. What attitudes toward money does Jesus urge in Luke 12?

12. Why is it easy for us to waste energy worrying about having enough stuff?

**In what one concrete way can you put God's Kingdom ahead of your own gain?**

13. In practical terms, how does a person go about seeking God's Kingdom ahead of seeking prosperity?

• • • • • • • • • • • • • • • • • • • • • • • • • • • • • • • • • • • • • • • • • • •

## RELIGIOUS LEADERS SURROUND JESUS AT THE TEMPLE *John 10:22-42*

*[22]Then came the Feast of Dedication at Jerusalem. It was winter, [23]and Jesus was in the temple area walking in Solomon's Colonnade. [24]The Jews gathered around him, saying, "How long will you keep us in*

suspense? If you are the Christ, tell us plainly."

<sup>25</sup>Jesus answered, "I did tell you, but you do not believe. The miracles I do in my Father's name speak for me, <sup>26</sup>but you do not believe because you are not my sheep. <sup>27</sup>My sheep listen to my voice; I know them, and they follow me. <sup>28</sup>I give them eternal life, and they shall never perish; no one can snatch them out of my hand. <sup>29</sup>My Father, who has given them to me, is greater than all; no one can snatch them out of my Father's hand. <sup>30</sup>I and the Father are one."

<sup>31</sup>Again the Jews picked up stones to stone him, <sup>32</sup>but Jesus said to them, "I have shown you many great miracles from the Father. For which of these do you stone me?"

<sup>33</sup>"We are not stoning you for any of these," replied the Jews, "but for blasphemy, because you, a mere man, claim to be God."

<sup>34</sup>Jesus answered them, "Is it not written in your Law, 'I have said you are gods'? <sup>35</sup>If he called them 'gods,' to whom the word of God came—and the Scripture cannot be broken—<sup>36</sup>what about the one whom the Father set apart as his very own and sent into the world? Why then do you accuse me of blasphemy because I said, 'I am God's Son'? <sup>37</sup>Do not believe me unless I do what my Father does. <sup>38</sup>But if I do it, even though you do not believe me, believe the miracles, that you may know and understand that the Father is in me, and I in the Father." <sup>39</sup>Again they tried to seize him, but he escaped their grasp.

<sup>40</sup>Then Jesus went back across the Jordan to the place where John had been baptizing in the early days. Here he stayed <sup>41</sup>and many people came to him. They said, "Though John never performed a miraculous sign, all that John said about this man was true." <sup>42</sup>And in that place many believed in Jesus. (John 10:22-42)

**They asked for it!** In response to the demands of the religious leaders, Jesus boldly declared that He was one with the Father. But they still refused to believe. Instead, they accused Him of blasphemy and tried once again to kill Him. Nothing Jesus said or did could convince them of the truth because they had hardened their hearts.

14. What reasons did Jesus give for the people to believe that He was the Christ?

15. Do you think these are the most important reasons? Why, or why not?

What biblical truths are most difficult for you to accept? Why?

16. Why is Jesus' message difficult for people to accept?

17. How do even obedient Christians sometimes harden their hearts to the truth of the gospel?

What is hindering your under-standing of or obedience to Christ's teaching?

**The truth is sometimes hard to swallow.** Just as the religious leaders refused to believe what Jesus said about them, it's often difficult for us to fully accept His teaching. We've learned in this lesson that pride, materialism, worry, and self-ishness can keep us from recognizing and accepting the truth. But if we keep our eyes fixed on Jesus, He will reveal the truths of His Kingdom to us.

How can you begin to eliminate this hindrance from your life?

# LESSON FIVE
# A TRUE FRIEND

One aspect of Jesus' life that is easy to over-look is His deliberate choice of friends. He didn't seek out the most educated, the best looking, or the wealthiest people. Instead, He befriended humble fishermen, poor women, lepers, prostitutes, and other social outcasts. This lesson will reveal what kind of friend Jesus was and what character traits He valued in others. You will learn from His example what it means to be a true friend.

## JESUS HEALS AND TEACHES PEOPLE
### Luke 13:22–14:24

²²Then Jesus went through the towns and villages, teaching as he made his way to Jerusalem. ²³Someone asked him, "Lord, are only a few people going to be saved?"

He said to them, ²⁴"Make every effort to enter through the narrow door, because many, I tell you, will try to enter and will not be able to. ²⁵Once the owner of the house gets up and closes the door, you will stand outside knocking and pleading, 'Sir, open the door for us.'

"But he will answer, 'I don't know you or where you come from.'

*For he will deliver the needy who cry out, the afflicted who have no one to help. He will take pity on the weak and the needy and save the needy from death. He will rescue them from oppression and violence, for precious is their blood in his sight.*
*(Psalm 72:12-14)*

²⁶"Then you will say, 'We ate and drank with you, and you taught in our streets.'

²⁷"But he will reply, 'I don't know you or where you come from. Away from me, all you evildoers!'

²⁸"There will be weeping there, and gnashing of teeth, when you see Abraham, Isaac and Jacob and all the prophets in the kingdom of God, but you yourselves thrown out. ²⁹People will come from east and west and north and south, and will take their places at the feast in the kingdom of God. ³⁰Indeed there are those who are last who will be first, and first who will be last."

³¹At that time some Pharisees came to Jesus and said to him, "Leave this place and go somewhere else. Herod wants to kill you."

³²He replied, "Go tell that fox, 'I will drive out demons and heal people today and tomorrow, and on the third day I will reach my goal.' ³³In any case, I must keep going today and tomorrow and the next day—for surely no prophet can die outside Jerusalem!

³⁴"O Jerusalem, Jerusalem, you who kill the prophets and stone those sent to you, how often I have longed to gather your children together, as a hen gathers her chicks under her wings, but you were not willing! ³⁵Look, your house is left to you desolate. I tell you, you will not see me again until you say, 'Blessed is he who comes in the name of the Lord.'"

¹One Sabbath, when Jesus went to eat in the house of a prominent Pharisee, he was being carefully watched. ²There in front of him was a man suffering from dropsy. ³Jesus asked the Pharisees and experts in the law, "Is it lawful to heal on the Sabbath or not?" ⁴But they remained silent. So taking hold of the man, he healed him and sent him away.

⁵Then he asked them, "If one of you has a son or an ox that falls into a well on the Sabbath day, will you not immediately pull him out?" ⁶And they had nothing to say.

⁷When he noticed how the guests picked the places of honor at the table, he told them this parable: ⁸"When someone invites you to a wedding

feast, do not take the place of honor, for a person more distinguished than you may have been invited. ⁹If so, the host who invited both of you will come and say to you, 'Give this man your seat.' Then, humiliated, you will have to take the least important place. ¹⁰But when you are invited, take the lowest place, so that when your host comes, he will say to you, 'Friend, move up to a better place.' Then you will be honored in the presence of all your fellow guests. ¹¹For everyone who exalts himself will be humbled, and he who humbles himself will be exalted."

¹²Then Jesus said to his host, "When you give a luncheon or dinner, do not invite your friends, your brothers or relatives, or your rich neighbors; if you do, they may invite you back and so you will be repaid. ¹³But when you give a banquet, invite the poor, the crippled, the lame, the blind, ¹⁴and you will be blessed. Although they cannot repay you, you will be repaid at the resurrection of the righteous."

¹⁵When one of those at the table with him heard this, he said to Jesus, "Blessed is the man who will eat at the feast in the kingdom of God."

¹⁶Jesus replied: "A certain man was preparing a great banquet and invited many guests. ¹⁷At the time of the banquet he sent his servant to tell those who had been invited, 'Come, for everything is now ready.'

¹⁸"But they all alike began to make excuses. The first said, 'I have just bought a field, and I must go and see it. Please excuse me.'

¹⁹"Another said, 'I have just bought five yoke of oxen, and I'm on my way to try them out. Please excuse me.'

²⁰"Still another said, 'I just got married, so I can't come.'

²¹"The servant came back and reported this to his master. Then the owner of the house became angry and ordered his servant, 'Go out quickly into the streets and alleys of the town and bring in the poor, the crippled, the blind and the lame.'

²²"'Sir,' the servant said, 'what you ordered has been done, but there is still room.'

*²³"Then the master told his servant, 'Go out to the roads and country lanes and make them come in, so that my house will be full. ²⁴I tell you, not one of those men who were invited will get a taste of my banquet.'"* (Luke 13:22–14:24)

**When Jesus saw the guests fighting** over the best seats at this dinner party, He told them a parable that revealed the importance of humility. Rather than seeking status and success, Jesus tells us to serve Him. This means giving to people who cannot repay us and helping others when no one else is looking. Jesus promises that those who have humbled themselves in this life will be exalted in the Kingdom of Heaven.

1. While in the Pharisee's home, Jesus taught three subjects. As you study Luke 14, record what stimulated Jesus to speak, His main point, and the response He calls for.

   Luke 14:7-11

   Luke 14:12-14

2. How do you think the guests rationalized seeking the places of honor?

3. How can we know if we pay too much attention to wealth, power, and status?

4. What kind of people does Jesus want us to serve?

Who is one person
you could serve
this week?

5. Why serve those people?

• • • • • • • • • • • • • • • • • • • • • • • • • • • • • • • • • • • • • •
## JESUS TEACHES ABOUT THE COST OF BEING A DISCIPLE *Luke 14:25-35*

[25]*Large crowds were traveling with Jesus, and turning to them he said:* [26]*"If anyone comes to me and does not hate his father and mother, his wife and children, his brothers and sisters—yes, even his own life—he cannot be my disciple.* [27]*And anyone who does not carry his cross and follow me cannot be my disciple.*

[28]*"Suppose one of you wants to build a tower. Will he not first sit down and estimate the cost to see if he has enough money to complete it?* [29]*For if he lays the foundation and is not able to finish it, everyone who sees it will ridicule him,* [30]*saying, 'This fellow began to build and was not able to finish.'*

[31]*"Or suppose a king is about to go to war against another king. Will he not first sit down and consider whether he is able with ten thousand men to oppose the one coming against him with twenty thousand?* [32]*If he is not able, he will send a delegation while the other is still a long way off and will ask for terms of peace.* [33]*In the same way, any of you who does not give up everything he has cannot be my disciple.*

[34]*"Salt is good, but if it loses its saltiness, how can it be made salty again?* [35]*It is fit neither for the soil nor for the manure pile; it is thrown out.*

*"He who has ears to hear, let him hear."* (Luke 14:25-35)

**Earlier in His ministry,** Jesus taught about discipleship. But now He clearly spelled out the conditions for being a true disciple. He wanted the people to carefully consider the cost of following Him because He didn't want half-hearted followers. He knew that their enthusiasm would soon evaporate as He faced the cross instead of the throne that the Jews expected.

6. What prerequisites did Jesus set for His disciples?

How do the requirements in this passage apply to us today?

7. What does Jesus mean when He tells us to "hate" our parents, spouse, children, and siblings?

What sacrifices are most difficult for you to make to follow Christ?

8. What do Jesus' examples of building a tower and preparing for war teach us about following Him?

What steps could
you take this week
to strengthen your
loyalty to Christ?

9. Why do you think Jesus set such stringent
standards?

• • • • • • • • • • • • • • • • • • • • • • • • • • • • • • • • • • • • •

## JESUS TELLS THREE PARABLES
### Luke 15:1-32

¹*Now the tax collectors and "sinners" were all
gathering around to hear him. ²But the Pharisees
and the teachers of the law muttered, "This man
welcomes sinners and eats with them."*

³*Then Jesus told them this parable:* ⁴*"Suppose
one of you has a hundred sheep and loses one of
them. Does he not leave the ninety-nine in the open
country and go after the lost sheep until he finds it?
⁵And when he finds it, he joyfully puts it on his
shoulders ⁶and goes home. Then he calls his friends
and neighbors together and says, 'Rejoice with me;
I have found my lost sheep.' ⁷I tell you that in the
same way there will be more rejoicing in heaven
over one sinner who repents than over ninety-nine
righteous persons who do not need to repent.*

⁸*"Or suppose a woman has ten silver coins and
loses one. Does she not light a lamp, sweep the
house and search carefully until she finds it? ⁹And
when she finds it, she calls her friends and neighbors together and says, 'Rejoice with me; I have
found my lost coin.' ¹⁰In the same way, I tell you,
there is rejoicing in the presence of the angels of
God over one sinner who repents."*

¹¹*Jesus continued: "There was a man who had
two sons. ¹²The younger one said to his father,
'Father, give me my share of the estate.' So he
divided his property between them.*

¹³*"Not long after that, the younger son got*

together all he had, set off for a distant country and there squandered his wealth in wild living. ¹⁴After he had spent everything, there was a severe famine in that whole country, and he began to be in need. ¹⁵So he went and hired himself out to a citizen of that country, who sent him to his fields to feed pigs. ¹⁶He longed to fill his stomach with the pods that the pigs were eating, but no one gave him anything.

¹⁷"When he came to his senses, he said, 'How many of my father's hired men have food to spare, and here I am starving to death! ¹⁸I will set out and go back to my father and say to him: Father, I have sinned against heaven and against you. ¹⁹I am no longer worthy to be called your son; make me like one of your hired men.' ²⁰So he got up and went to his father.

"But while he was still a long way off, his father saw him and was filled with compassion for him; he ran to his son, threw his arms around him and kissed him.

²¹"The son said to him, 'Father, I have sinned against heaven and against you. I am no longer worthy to be called your son.'

²²"But the father said to his servants, 'Quick! Bring the best robe and put it on him. Put a ring on his finger and sandals on his feet. ²³Bring the fattened calf and kill it. Let's have a feast and celebrate. ²⁴For this son of mine was dead and is alive again; he was lost and is found.' So they began to celebrate.

²⁵"Meanwhile, the older son was in the field. When he came near the house, he heard music and dancing. ²⁶So he called one of the servants and asked him what was going on. ²⁷'Your brother has come,' he replied, 'and your father has killed the fattened calf because he has him back safe and sound.'

²⁸"The older brother became angry and refused to go in. So his father went out and pleaded with him. ²⁹But he answered his father, 'Look! All these years I've been slaving for you and never disobeyed your orders. Yet you never gave me even a young goat so I could celebrate with my friends. ³⁰But

*when this son of yours who has squandered your property with prostitutes comes home, you kill the fattened calf for him!'*

*31"'My son,' the father said, 'you are always with me, and everything I have is yours. 32But we had to celebrate and be glad, because this brother of yours was dead and is alive again; he was lost and is found.'"* (Luke 15:1-32)

Jesus taught a mixed crowd—His disciples, the outcasts of society, and the religious leaders from Jerusalem. When the Pharisees complained about His association with "sinners," Jesus told three parables to explain that God's love is for everyone. The teachers of the law had written off many people as lost cases, but Jesus wanted to welcome these lost sheep into the Kingdom of God.

How does it make you feel to know there is "rejoicing in heaven" each time a person repents?

10. What do these parables reveal about the Kingdom of God?

How have you personally experienced God's forgiveness?

11. How does God treat people differently than we do?

12. What responsibility do we have to people who have not accepted Christ?

In light of these parables, how do you think God would want you to treat people differently?

13. In what ways can you identify with the younger son in the third parable?

How can you thank God today for His love and forgiveness?

14. In what ways can you identify with the older son?

**Unlike the Pharisees, Jesus loved sinners.** He went out of His way to befriend people the Pharisees refused to touch. Jesus loves all of us, despite our past mistakes. Instead of treating us as we deserve, He loves and forgives us. Jesus challenges us to follow His example — this means looking past people's appearances, reputations, and shortcomings and being a true friend.

How can you show Christlike love and compassion to a friend this week?

# HARMONY OF THE LIFE AND MINISTRY OF JESUS CHRIST

| | MATTHEW | MARK | LUKE | JOHN |
|---|---|---|---|---|
| | *THE BEGINNING* | | | |
| **LESSON 1** | *The men who wrote the Gospels*<br>1:1 | | 1:1-4 | |
| | *God became a human being* | | | 1:1-18 |
| | *The ancestors of Jesus*<br>1:1-17 | | 3:23-38 | |
| **LESSON 2** | *An angel promises the birth of John to Zechariah* | | 1:5-25 | |
| | *An angel promises the birth of Jesus to Mary* | | 1:26-38 | |
| | *Mary visits Elizabeth* | | 1:39-56 | |
| | *John the Baptist is born* | | 1:57-80 | |
| **LESSON 3** | *An angel appears to Joseph*<br>1:18-25 | | | |
| | *Jesus is born* | | 2:1-20 | |
| | *Mary and Joseph bring Jesus to the temple* | | 2:21-40 | |
| | *Visitors arrive from eastern lands*<br>2:1-12 | | | |
| | *The escape to Egypt and return to Nazareth*<br>2:13-23 | | | |
| | *Jesus' youth* | | 2:41-52 | |
| **LESSON 4** | *John the Baptist prepares the way for Jesus*<br>3:1-12 | 1:2-8 | 3:1-20 | 1:19-28 |
| | *John baptizes Jesus*<br>3:13-17 | 1:9-11 | 3:21-22 | 1:29-34 |
| | *Satan tempts Jesus in the desert*<br>4:1-11 | 1:12-13 | 4:1-13 | |
| | *The first disciples follow Jesus* | | | 1:35-51 |

| | MATTHEW | MARK | LUKE | JOHN |
|---|---|---|---|---|
| **LESSON 5** | *Jesus turns water into wine* | | | 2:1-11 |
| | *Jesus clears the temple* | | | 2:12-25 |
| | *Nicodemus visits Jesus at night* | | | 3:1-21 |
| | *John the Baptist tells more about Jesus* | | | 3:22-36 |

## CHALLENGING TRADITION

| | MATTHEW | MARK | LUKE | JOHN |
|---|---|---|---|---|
| **LESSON 1** | *The Samaritan woman believes in Jesus* | | | 4:1-42 |
| | *Jesus preaches in Galilee*<br>4:12 | 1:14-15 | 4:14-15 | 4:43-45 |
| | *Jesus heals a government official's son* | | | 4:46-54 |
| | *Jesus is rejected at Nazareth* | | 4:16-30 | |
| **LESSON 2** | *Jesus moves to Capernaum*<br>4:13-17 | | 4:31 | |
| | *Four fisherman follow Jesus*<br>4:18-22 | 1:16-20 | 5:1-11 | |
| | *Jesus heals and teaches people*<br>4:23-25;<br>8:1-4,14-17;<br>9:1-8 | 1:21–2:12 | 4:33-44,<br>5:12-26 | |
| | *Jesus eats with sinners at Matthew's house*<br>9:9-13 | 2:13-17 | 5:27-32 | |
| **LESSON 3** | *Religious leaders ask Jesus about fasting*<br>9:14-17 | 2:18-22 | 5:33-39 | |
| | *Jesus heals people on the Sabbath*<br>12:1-21 | 2:23–3:12 | 6:1-11 | 5:1-47 |
| | *Jesus selects the twelve disciples*<br>10:2-4 | 3:13-19 | 6:12-16 | |
| | *Jesus gives the Beatitudes*<br>5:1-16 | | 6:17-26 | |
| | *Jesus teaches about the law*<br>5:17-48 | | 6:27-36 | |

| | MATTHEW | MARK | LUKE | JOHN |
|---|---|---|---|---|
| **LESSON 4** | *Jesus teaches about giving and prayer*<br>6:1-8,<br>6:16–7:12 | | 6:37-42 | |
| | *Jesus teaches about the way to Heaven*<br>7:13-29 | | 6:43-49 | |
| | *A Roman centurion demonstrates faith*<br>8:5-13 | | 7:1-10 | |
| | *Jesus raises a widow's son from the dead* | | 7:11-17 | |
| **LESSON 5** | *Jesus eases John's doubt*<br>11:1-30 | | 7:18-35 | |
| | *A sinful woman anoints Jesus' feet* | | 7:36–8:3 | |
| | *Religious leaders falsely accuse Jesus*<br>12:22-45 | 3:20-30 | 11:14-28 | |
| | *Jesus describes His true family*<br>12:46-50 | 3:31-35 | 8:19-21 | |
| | *THE MESSIAH* | | | |
| **LESSON 1** | *Jesus teaches through parables*<br>13:1-52 | 4:1-34 | 8:4-18 | |
| | *Jesus calms the storm*<br>8:23-27 | 4:35-41 | 8:22-25 | |
| | *Jesus sends the demons into a herd of pigs*<br>8:28-34 | 5:1-20 | 8:26-39 | |
| | *Jesus heals people and raises a girl to life*<br>9:18-34 | 5:21-43 | 8:40-56 | |
| **LESSON 2** | *The people of Nazareth refuse to believe*<br>13:53-58 | 6:1-6 | | |
| | *Jesus sends out the twelve disciples*<br>9:35–10:42 | 6:7-13 | 9:1-6 | |
| | *Herod kills John the Baptist*<br>14:1-12 | 6:14-29 | 9:7-9 | |
| | *Jesus feeds the five thousand*<br>14:13-21 | 6:30-44 | 9:10-17 | 6:1-15 |

| | MATTHEW | MARK | LUKE | JOHN |
|---|---|---|---|---|
| **LESSON 3** | *Jesus walks on water*<br>14:22-36 | 6:45-56 | | 6:16-21 |
| | *Jesus is the true bread from Heaven* | | | 6:22-71 |
| | *Jesus teaches about inner purity*<br>15:1-20 | 7:1-23 | | |
| | *Jesus sends a demon out of a girl*<br>15:21-28 | 7:24-30 | | |
| | *Jesus feeds four thousand*<br>15:29-39 | 7:31–8:10 | | |
| **LESSON 4** | *Religious leaders ask for a sign in the sky*<br>16:1-12 | 8:11-21 | | |
| | *Jesus restores sight to a blind man* | 8:22-26 | | |
| | *Peter says Jesus is the Messiah*<br>16:13-20 | 8:27-30 | 9:18-20 | |
| | *Jesus predicts His death the first time*<br>16:21-28 | 8:31–9:1 | 9:21-27 | |
| **LESSON 5** | *Jesus is transfigured on the mountain*<br>17:1-13 | 9:2-13 | 9:28-36 | |
| | *Jesus heals a demon-possessed boy*<br>17:14-21 | 9:14-29 | 9:37-43 | |
| | *Jesus predicts His death the second time*<br>17:22-23 | 9:30-32 | 9:44-45 | |
| | *Peter finds the coin in the fish's mouth*<br>17:24-27 | | | |
| | | *FOLLOWING JESUS* | | |
| **LESSON 1** | *Jesus warns against temptation*<br>18:1-35 | 9:33-50 | 9:46-50 | |
| | *Jesus teaches about the cost of following Him*<br>8:18-22,<br>19:1-2 | 10:1 | 9:51-62 | 7:2-9 |
| | *Jesus teaches openly at the temple* | | | 7:10-53 |
| **LESSON 2** | *Jesus forgives an adulterous woman* | | | 8:1-11 |
| | *Jesus teaches about Himself* | | | 8:12-59 |
| | *Jesus heals a blind man* | | | 9:1-41 |

| | MATTHEW | MARK | LUKE | JOHN |
|---|---|---|---|---|
| **LESSON 3** | Jesus is the good shepherd | | | 10:1-21 |
| | Jesus sends out seventy-two messengers | | 10:1-24 | |
| | Jesus tells the parable of the good Samaritan | | 10:25-37 | |
| | Jesus visits Mary and Martha | | 10:38-42 | |
| **LESSON 4** | Jesus teaches His disciples about prayer 6:9-15 | | 11:1-13 | |
| | Jesus exposes the religious leaders | | 11:37–12:12 | |
| | Jesus warns the people | | 12:13–13:21 | |
| | Religious leaders surround Jesus at the temple | | | 10:22-42 |
| **LESSON 5** | Jesus heals and teaches people | | 13:22–14:24 | |
| | Jesus teaches about the cost of being a disciple | | 14:25-35 | |
| | Jesus tells three parables | | 15:1-32 | |
| | ANSWERING THE CALL | | | |
| **LESSON 1** | Jesus teaches His disciples | | 16:1–17:10 | |
| | Jesus raises Lazarus from the dead | | | 11:1-44 |
| | Jesus heals ten men with leprosy | | 17:11-19 | |
| **LESSON 2** | Jesus teaches about the Kingdom of God | | 17:20-37 | |
| | Jesus tells two parables on prayer | | 18:1-14 | |
| | Jesus teaches about marriage and divorce 19:3-12 | 10:2-12 | | |
| | Jesus blesses little children 19:13-15 | 10:13-16 | 18:15-17 | |

| | MATTHEW | MARK | LUKE | JOHN |
|---|---|---|---|---|
| **LESSON 3** | *Jesus speaks to the rich young man*<br>19:16–20:16 | 10:17-31 | 18:18-30 | |
| | *Jesus teaches about serving others*<br>20:17-28 | 10:32-45 | 18:31-34 | |
| | *Jesus heals a blind beggar*<br>20:29-34 | 10:46-52 | 18:35-43 | |
| **LESSON 4** | *Jesus brings salvation to Zacchaeus's home* | | 19:1-10 | |
| | *Jesus tells the parable of the king's ten servants* | | 19:11-27 | |
| | *Religious leaders plot to kill Jesus* | | | 11:45-57,<br>12:9-11 |
| | *Jesus rides into Jerusalem on a donkey*<br>21:1-11,14-17 | 11:1-11 | 19:28-44 | 12:12-13 |
| **LESSON 5** | *Jesus curses the fig tree*<br>21:18-19 | 11:12-14 | | |
| | *Jesus clears the temple again*<br>21:12-13 | 11:15-19 | 19:45-48 | |
| | *Jesus summarizes His purpose and message* | | | 12:20-50 |
| | *Jesus says His disciples can pray for anything*<br>21:20-22 | 11:20-25 | | |

## FINAL TEACHINGS

| | MATTHEW | MARK | LUKE | JOHN |
|---|---|---|---|---|
| **LESSON 1** | *Religious leaders challenge Jesus' authority*<br>21:23-27 | 11:27-33 | 20:1-8 | |
| | *Jesus tells three parables*<br>21:28–22:14 | 12:1-12 | 20:9-19 | |
| | *Religious leaders ask Jesus three questions*<br>22:15-40 | 12:13-34 | 20:20-40 | |
| | *Religious leaders cannot answer Jesus' question*<br>22:41-46 | 12:35-37 | 20:41-44 | |
| **LESSON 2** | *Jesus warns against the religious leaders*<br>23:1-12 | 12:38-40 | 20:45-47 | |
| | *Jesus condemns the religious leaders*<br>23:13-39 | | | |
| | *A poor widow gives all she has* | 12:41-44 | 21:1-4 | |
| | *Jesus tells about the future*<br>24:1-51 | 13:1-37 | 21:5-38 | |

| | Event | MATTHEW | MARK | LUKE | JOHN |
|---|---|---|---|---|---|
| **LESSON 3** | Jesus tells about the final judgment | 25:1-46 | | | |
| | Religious leaders plot to kill Jesus | 26:1-5 | 14:1-2 | 22:1-2 | |
| | A woman anoints Jesus with perfume | 26:6-13 | 14:3-9 | | 12:1-8 |
| | Judas agrees to betray Jesus | 26:14-16 | 14:10-11 | 22:3-6 | |
| **LESSON 4** | Disciples prepare for the Passover | 26:17-19 | 14:12-16 | 22:7-13 | |
| | Jesus washes His disciples' feet | | | | 13:1-20 |
| | Jesus foretells His betrayal and suffering | 26:20-25 | 14:17-21 | 22:14-16,21-30 | 13:21-30 |
| **LESSON 5** | Jesus and His disciples have the Last Supper | 26:26-28 | 14:22-24 | 22:17-20 | |
| | Jesus talks with His disciples about the future | 26:29-30 | 14:25-26 | | 13:31–14:31 |
| | Jesus predicts Peter's denial | 26:31-35 | 14:27-31 | 22:31-38 | |
| | Jesus teaches about the vine and the branches | | | | 15:1–16:4 |

## THE CROSS AND THE RESURRECTION

| | Event | MATTHEW | MARK | LUKE | JOHN |
|---|---|---|---|---|---|
| **LESSON 1** | Jesus teaches about the Holy Spirit and prayer | | | | 16:5-33 |
| | Jesus prays for Himself and believers | | | | 17:1-26 |
| | Jesus agonizes in the garden | 26:36-46 | 14:32-42 | 22:39-46 | 18:1 |
| | Jesus is betrayed and arrested | 26:47-56 | 14:43-52 | 22:47-53 | 18:2-11 |
| **LESSON 2** | Jesus is questioned and condemned | 26:57,59-68, 27:1 | 14:53,55-65, 15:1 | 22:54,63-71 | 18:12-14,19-24 |
| | Peter denies knowing Jesus | 26:58,69-75 | 14:54,66-72 | 22:54-62 | 18:15-18,25-27 |
| | Judas kills himself (see also Acts 1:18-19) | 27:3-10 | | | |
| | Jesus stands trial before Pilate and Herod | 27:2,11-31 | 15:1-20 | 23:1-25 | 18:28–19:16 |

| | MATTHEW | MARK | LUKE | JOHN |
|---|---|---|---|---|
| **LESSON 3** | *Jesus is crucified*<br>27:31-56 | 15:20-41 | 23:26-49 | 19:16-37 |
| | *Jesus is buried*<br>27:57-66 | 15:42-47 | 23:50-56 | 19:38-42 |
| | *Jesus rises from the dead and appears to the women*<br>28:1-15 | 16:1-11 | 24:1-12 | 20:1-18 |
| **LESSON 4** | *Jesus appears to two believers traveling on the road*<br> | 16:12-13 | 24:13-35 | |
| | *Jesus appears to the disciples behind locked doors*<br> | 16:14 | 24:36-43 | 20:19-23 |
| | *Jesus appears to the disciples, including Thomas* | | | 20:24-31 |
| | *Jesus appears to the disciples while fishing* | | | 21:1-25 |
| **LESSON 5** | *Jesus gives the Great Commission*<br>28:16-20 | 16:15-18 | | |
| | *Jesus appears to the disciples in Jerusalem*  (see also Acts 1:3-8) | | 24:44-49 | |
| | *Jesus ascends into Heaven*  (see also Acts 1:9-12)<br> | 16:19-20 | 24:50-53 | |